Original title:
The Joys of Not Knowing the Meaning of Life

Copyright © 2025 Creative Arts Management OÜ
All rights reserved.

Author: Amelia Montgomery
ISBN HARDBACK: 978-1-80566-105-4
ISBN PAPERBACK: 978-1-80566-400-0

Lifting Veils of Fascination

In a world where questions swirl,
I dance with confusion's twirl.
Why is the sky, blue or gray?
I'll just pretend it's a buffet!

Cats are plotting world domination,
While I'm lost in daydreams' station.
Why do we laugh? Why do we cry?
Let's just blame it on the pie!

I question life like it's a book,
But it's more a cosmic cook.
With recipes for smiles and strife,
Missing the point—oh, what a life!

In every riddle, joy pursues,
With a side of spicy news.
Who needs answers, really friend?
Let's toast to questions with no end!

Embracing the Dance of Uncertainty

Twist like a pretzel, sway with delight,
Who needs a map on this whimsical flight?
Step on my toes, I'll laugh in the fray,
Each clueless jig adds a bounce to the day.

With socks that don't match, I shuffle around,
In the chaos of laughter, my joy can be found.
Why follow a script? Let the music just flow,
The dance of confusion is quite the show!

Secrets Hidden in Everyday Smiles

A wink from the barista, a nod from the cat,
What is the message? I ponder and chat.
With each goofy grin, a balance we strike,
Life's little puzzles? A delightful hike.

The man with the hat drops some crumbs on the floor,
Is it breadcrumbs to wisdom or just leftover s'mores?
A smile is a mystery, an enigma wrapped tight,
In the theater of nonsense, we bask in delight.

The Freedom Found in Letting Go

Tossing my worries like stones in a brook,
With each splash of laughter, I tease and I look.
What if I tumbled over thoughts in my head?
At least I'd land softly on laughter instead!

My shoes all untied, rhythm lacking in grace,
Yet somehow I dance with a joy on my face.
In a world without answers, a blissful release,
I tumble and giggle, and that brings me peace.

Joyful Stumbles on the Road of Life

Road trips with no map, just snacks and a song,
Each bump and each turn, it all feels so wrong.
But laughter erupts like a bright summer rain,
As we swerve past confusion, what's there to gain?

With friends by my side, all our plans go awry,
Yet in the madness, we all touch the sky.
In stumbles and fumbles, our hearts start to glow,
The best kind of journey is one where we flow.

A Garden of Mysterious Paths

In a garden where daisies laugh,
I took a stroll on a crooked path.
The signs were missing, oh what a joke,
I followed a squirrel, it led to smoke.

Sunflowers spinning like they knew best,
Giggling secrets, they put me to test.
Why chase the answers, when fun's all around?
I found a lost shoe, it was time to clown.

Savoring the Unscripted Moments

I ordered a coffee that came with a hat,
The barista grinned, not sure where I sat.
My sandwich performed like a Broadway star,
Each bite left me guessing where we really are.

Laughter erupts at a burbling stream,
What's life's purpose? Not sure, but I dream.
With every misstep, the world feels more bright,
I'll dance in the chaos, from morning to night.

The Beauty of the Unexplained

A cat in a bowtie just gave me a wink,
With polka dot socks, I questioned my drink.
Is this the cure for a serious face?
Or merely a stop in a comical race?

The clouds shape-shift into elephants grand,
I toss out my worries like grains of sand.
With giggles and wiggles, we float through the air,
No map in my pocket; do I really care?

Revelations in Confusion

A potato danced on the table with grace,
I laughed till I cried, what a curious place!
The fruit sang a song, I joined in the cheer,
Who needs an answer when laughter is near?

In puzzling moments, I glean all the fun,
I chased a lost thought, and we started to run.
With whimsy and wonder, life's a grand show,
Each twist is a punchline, come on, let's go!

Contentment in the Mystery of Being

With socks mispaired and coffee cold,
I wander through tales yet untold.
I trip on thoughts, a jumbled spree,
Ah, but what is that to me?

Each day a puzzle, pieces scatter,
The world spins round, and I just chatter.
Why fret for answers locked away?
I'll dance through night, and laugh all day.

Chasing Fireflies in a Darkened Wood

In twilight's grip, I sway and swish,
Pondering life, not one clear wish.
Fireflies blink like secrets bright,
Do they know what's wrong or right?

I gallivant through shadows deep,
Where mysteries whisper, and giggles creep.
With each elusive glow I dart,
Unraveled threads, a wiggly art.

Uncharted Paths of Existence

I've lost my way, but who can tell?
Every avenue's a cheeky spell.
With every turn a silly jest,
Life's playground swings, I take the rest.

Maps crumpled, GPS on mute,
Chasing dreams in mismatched boots.
In every folly, a spark of glee,
What's the end? Oh, let it be!

Reveling in the Unknown

With pie on my face, I greet the dawn,
Life's a circus, I'm the silly swan.
Questions fly like kites in the breeze,
But I'm too busy just to sneeze.

Hiccups of fate, a giggling thief,
Stealing sense, and leaving grief.
With every quirk and playful jest,
What's the plan? I'll just guess!

Reality in Fragments

In pieces we dance, a jig on the floor,
Trying to find what we all are here for.
With questions like bubbles, they pop in the air,
We giggle and wonder, do we really care?

Like socks gone missing, our thoughts drift apart,
A game of charades played by the heart.
Embrace the absurd, let the nonsense unfurl,
Life's like a pop quiz — let's give it a whirl!

Unwritten Stories of Existence

Each moment a page, scribbled hastily,
Characters laughing, like wildbirds, set free.
Plot twists aplenty, with each turn of fate,
The punchline's elusive, but isn't it great?

We're scribbling notes on a napkin or two,
In cafés where meaning slips right out of view.
Why nail down the answers when joy's in the play?
Let's write our own tales in the quirkiest way!

Laughter Echoes in the Silence

In the stillness, hear giggles that ring,
As questions loom large, like a cat on the swing.
With puzzled expressions and winks in between,
We manage to dance like we've lost all routine.

The mind throws confetti, a carnival sound,
Each thought's an adventure, we twirl all around.
No map for the journey, just follow the fun,
When laughter's the language, we all are as one!

Chasing Flickers of Possibility

Chase shadows of thoughts like they're fireflies bright,
Collecting their glimmers on warm summer nights.
What's this grand puzzle, a riddle, a jest?
In the chase, find the joy — isn't that our best?

With bright colored dreams that twist, turn, and soar,
Whimsy will guide us, let's open that door.
Life's not a ledger, it's a colorful spree,
In pursuit of the fun, we'll each find our key!

The Lightness of Unmeaning

In a world so bright and vast,
I trip on thoughts that never last.
Why does the toaster burn my bread?
Maybe it thinks I'm better dead!

Chasing dreams without a map,
I find comfort in the gap.
Is it foolish? Oh, perhaps!
But who needs sense? I'll take my naps!

I search for answers, but they hide,
Like socks that stroll out with the tide.
Life's a riddle, a playful tease,
I laugh at fate with utmost ease!

So here I bounce from doubt to cheer,
Wearing joy like a shiny sphere.
In the chaos, I find my song,
That says I've been right all along!

Flights of Fancy in the Unknown

Oh, what is life? A bird in flight,
Or maybe just a pizza bite?
I ponder deep, or maybe not,
While accidentally burning pot.

Answers are like socks on a spree,
Eluding me like a fleeting bee.
Do I care? I take a sip,
Of lemonade that's on my lip!

I see the stars, they wink and glow,
Like they hold secrets we'll never know.
Maybe they just want to jest,
And join me on this silly quest!

With laughter as my trusty guide,
I flip the questions, they abide.
In this circus of the bizarre,
I'll ride my dreams—let's go too far!

A Tapestry of Unanswered Whys

Here I sit in a cozy chair,
Wondering why I've got no hair.
Are my thoughts like socks in a wash?
Tangled up like a silly squash!

Questions spiral, collide, and sway,
Like kids on swings at the end of May.
Why does my coffee taste like shoe?
Guess it's a blend of 'What's my cue?'

A tapestry weaved with silly threads,
Of funny memes and half-baked spreads.
I giggle as I chase the light,
While pondering why I act contrite!

In this chaos, I find my peace,
The art of absurd, it will never cease.
So here's to life, that unknown spree,
Let's toast to confusion—just you and me!

Sipping the Elixir of the Unseen

With a cup of joy, I raise a toast,
To the mysteries I ponder the most.
I sip the elixir, what could it be?
An unanswered riddle, just like me!

The sun is a circus, the moon a clown,
With no directions, I just spin round.
Questions bubble like a fizzy drink,
And I drink deeply, too lost to think!

What is life? A cosmic game?
With rules that change and never claim.
I trip on giggles, I spill my cheer,
Dancing on dreams, no need to steer!

So let's embrace what's vague and sly,
With a wink to the stars and a cheerful sigh.
In the end, it's all about the fun,
In this grand play, we're all just one!

Reveling in Life's Inconsistencies

I searched for answers, found a frog,
It croaked a tune, as I scratched my nog.
A map I drew with crayons bright,
Led me to cake, what a lovely sight.

The stars above, they twinkle strange,
Constellations twist, like they're playing games.
With every guess, I trip and fall,
Yet laughter bubbles, through it all.

A wise old tree gave a shrug and yawn,
Said, "Life's a joke, wake up at dawn!"
When questions dance like fireflies,
I just sit back, enjoying the surprise.

In the circus of life, I take a seat,
Juggling thoughts, both silly and sweet.
Who needs a map or defined design?
I'll savor the chaos—it's quite divine!

Embracing the Mystique of Being

Oh life, you're like a box of socks,
Some odd, some striped, all in knots.
I wore mismatched shoes, on purpose, I swear,
Just to confuse, and give folks a scare.

A chicken crossed, but reason was lost,
Was it seeking truth, or just at a cost?
With questions bobbing like balloons in the sky,
I float along, just asking why.

Found wisdom tucked in a cereal bowl,
A fortune cookie claims it has a goal.
It told me to dance in my pajamas wide,
So I twirled in laughter, no shame I tried.

Life's quirks are gems, sparkly and bold,
Each day a riddle, a tale to be told.
I raise my glass to the perplexity,
With each sip, I toast to absurdity!

The Light of Unsought Paths

Wandered down roads paved with cheer,
Found a clown just pulling my ear.
"Where are we going?" I cried in jest,
He honked his nose, said, "Go with the rest!"

A map made of jelly, sticky and bright,
Led me to nowhere, oh what a sight!
In every twist, a giggle's found,
Life's like a dance, so silly and round.

A cactus spoke, with spines on edge,
"Embrace the prickles, jump off the ledge!"
I laughed so hard, tears filled my eyes,
Who needs the answers when fun's the prize?

With each step taken, I trip and sway,
Life's a grand game, let's play it my way.
No need for compass or guiding light,
Just follow the chuckles into the night!

Celebrating Ambiguous Dawn

The sun's not sure if it's night or day,
It peeks and giggles, then runs away.
With breakfast thoughts that seem quite bizarre,
I'd rather sip dreams from a quirky jar.

Clouds play peek-a-boo with the moon,
While squirrels argue about their afternoon.
In this whirling dance of oddity and cheer,
I chuckle and wander, no worries near.

A raindrop asked, "Why can't I flow?"
I answered back, "Just let it go!"
With puddles splashed, reflections blimp,
Life's a jigsaw, just enjoy the imp.

So let's toast to morning's confused start,
With mismatched mugs and a goofy heart.
For in this riddle wrapped in delight,
Not knowing is fun, so hold on tight!

Cherishing Unsought Answers

A question marks the start of the day,
Like socks that don't match, it's here to stay.
Ignoring the riddle that life tossed my way,
I giggle and grin, come what may!

With each twist of fate, my coffee spills,
It's a cosmic joke, filled with playful frills.
Like cats on a trampoline, dancing with thrills,
I cherish the chaos, it's part of the drills.

In search of the map, but what's become clear,
Is I'm lost in the laughter, and that's quite dear.
Like socks, mismatched, but oh-so sincere,
I clink my cup and toast with cheer!

So hand me confusion, mixed thoughts in a bowl,
I'll stir it with joy, and let good times roll.
In this circus of life, I'm playing my role,
A banana peel slip can make the heart whole!

A Quest for the Unseekable

I set out one day on a grand, noble quest,
To find what's elusive, the truth manifest.
But the only compass in hand was my jest,
Leading me straight to a comedic fest!

With pop-tarts for armor, I marched through the streets,
While dodging the inquiries, I danced on my feet.
For wisdom can hide in the silliest treats,
Like fishing for meaning with gumdrop fleets.

The echoes of laughter soon filled up the air,
As I stumbled through puzzles without any care.
Conundrums and quandaries, I gleefully wear,
Like a woeful magician caught in a snare.

In the chaos of queries, I found a delight,
Like a squirrel that twirls in the shimmering light.
With riddles unbent and futures so bright,
I embraced the unknown, with pure childlike slight!

Freedom in Formlessness

In a world full of shapes, I embrace the free round,
Like a jellybean bouncing, no boundaries found.
Each tumble and twist is a power unbound,
With giggles of nonsense, and laughter profound!

Who needs a straight path, when curves bring the fun?
Like popcorn at parties, life's never been done.
With silliness reign, I'm both poet and pun,
In whimsy, I bask, chasing rays from the sun.

I spread out my arms, let the chaos erupt,
Like a spaghetti tornado, I welcome the uncupt.
For answers elusive can fill up my cup,
With sparkles of mayhem, I giggle, I erupt!

So here's to the wild, the weird, and the free,
Each nonsensical moment is a slice of glee.
In this form of formless, I finally see,
That life's fun house mirror is simply me!

Embracing Life's Grey Areas

In shades that confound, where colors collide,
I find joy in the grey, not wishing to hide.
With mismatched opinions and all that they bide,
A dance of the silly, in laughter, I glide.

Questions like jellybeans stuck in a jar,
I nibble and ponder, unsure of the star.
Yet every confusion leads me to bazaar,
Where humor bursts forth, leaving life in a spar.

There's freedom in vectors, the paths ever twist,
Like wearing a sandwich instead of a wrist.
With each tasty flop, it's a chance that I missed,
Yet love for the chaos, I can't help but insist!

For in the confounding, the mix and the mash,
I uncover the beauty, where worries can crash.
In giggles and grins, my thoughts come in a splash,
Embracing the unknowing, I live with panache!

The Dance of Uncertainty and Bliss

In a waltz with doubt, I twirl and sway,
Not knowing if I'm lost or found today.
The rhythm of chaos, a whimsical beat,
Life's a goofy dance with two left feet.

I trip on questions, laugh as I fall,
Who needs answers when confusion's a ball?
A jig where the punchlines never expire,
I juggle my thoughts, a chaotic choir.

With every misstep, I chuckle anew,
Dizzy with wonders, oh what fun to pursue!
Unraveled by riddles, I joyfully glide,
In this merry chaos, I take great pride.

So here's to the dance, to questions unkept,
We sip life's confusions, laughter adept.
In the grand masquerade of the great unknown,
I'll sway with delight, my heart is my throne.

Mosaic of the Unfamiliar

A patchwork of doubts, colorful and bright,
Each piece a mystery, a comical sight.
I stitch together giggles, and wonder flowing,
In this quirky canvas, creativity's glowing.

With every question mark, a splash of surprise,
Each puzzle unsolved brings lampooned highs.
Oh, the canvas of life is so splattered and bold,
A masterpiece forged with stories untold.

Lost and found in a jumble of thought,
In puzzles unbroken, I find joy in what's not.
The laughter erupts over shades in the art,
A gallery of whims, where joy claims its part.

So gather your pieces, let's paint on this chance,
We'll gleefully dance in this absurdist dance.
For wild, funny moments are treasures we find,
In the mosaic of life, we're all intertwined.

Secrets that Make Us Smile

There's a whisper of silliness hidden in air,
Like secrets that giggle beneath a wild stare.
Life's playful riddles wrapped tight in delight,
We chuckle in shadows, embracing the light.

What's the point of knowing when confusion feels grand?

A tangle of laughter, let's all take a stand.
With every quirked eyebrow and side-splitting jest,
We'll toast to the questions—unknowable, blessed!

With quirks in our pockets, we travel through jest,
In the game of livin', the smiles are the best.
Each giggle's a treasure, a charm we can use,
In the world of the baffled, we gladly amuse.

So lift a glass high to the nonsense we find,
In the secretive giggles that life leaves behind.
For every odd moment adds joy while we roam,
In this laughter-filled journey, we find our true home.

The Warmth of Ambiguous Emotions

A blanket of feelings, fuzzy and round,
Wrapped snug in the warmth where odd vibes abound.
With a side of confusion, I cozy right in,
In the melting pot of life, let the fun begin.

I play peek-a-boo with my thoughts, let them roam,
Like a cat in a bag, unsure of its home.
With smiles that bubble and frowns that dissolve,
In this wacky cocktail, my heart's sure to evolve.

Baffling by nature, we dive into glee,
With each twist and turn, the chuckles run free.
I sip on my feelings, a cocktail of zest,
In the blend of emotions, I find my quest.

So here's to the warmth of the whimsical ride,
Where the fluff of ambiguity tickles inside.
In the circus of feelings, I'll laugh 'til I cry,
For this vibrant confusion makes my soul fly.

The Sunshine of Disregarded Truths

With questions ricocheting in my head,
I dance through life with shoes of red.
Each answer slips, like butter on toast,
I laugh out loud, it's what I love most.

The map of facts is torn and worn,
I bumble on, barefoot and forlorn.
Who needs direction, I've lost my way,
I spin in circles and shout 'Hooray!'

Bright suns keep shining on things unknown,
While I chase shadows, I'm never alone.
Each twist and turn, a thrilling delight,
In my great adventure, all feels just right.

Here I am, content in my bliss,
Embracing the question, the sweet abyss.
For what's a life if answers aren't near?
Just me and the giggles, my only career.

Glee in Life's Mysteries

With mysteries folding like a paper plane,
I sail through skies, dance in the rain.
No compass to bind, just whims to explore,
In lands of the puzzled, I crave to be more.

How many licks to the center of truth?
I giggle and wonder, embracing my youth.
As puzzle pieces run off with the wind,
I collect silly moments, my life's greatest trend.

What's underneath all the stars in the dark?
I grin like a fox, it's all such a lark.
With every riddle tossed into the air,
I tumble and chuckle, without any care.

With joy in confusion and laughs in the night,
I swim in my thoughts, in pure delight.
So here's to the whimsies, the riddles we share,
In life's great show, it's a humorous flair!

Shadows of Happiness Spun

In shadows that dance, I muse and I chuckle,
Life's absurdities make my heart buckle.
Each twist and turn with a wink and a grin,
As I prance through puzzles, my joy comes from within.

Like a cat with a box, I ponder the night,
With no grand designs but feelings of light.
The jokes on the world are the best ones I find,
As happiness winks, leaving wisdom behind.

A circus of thoughts swirls up in my head,
With laughter as my blanket, snug on my bed.
Who needs clarity, or logical thought?
With glee in the game, I give it a shot.

So here's to the shadows that dance in the dark,
Each giggle a spark, each snort leaves a mark.
Let's skip through the fog and embrace the unknown,
For life's without meaning is where we have grown!

Moments Unconstrained by Meaning

With moments that giggle, like children at play,
I'll twirl through the paths, come what may.
Unfurling laughter in the wacky expanse,
Embracing each foolish, delightful chance.

Why ponder the why, when I can just be?
In wild little dances, I'm truly set free.
The clock chimes without reason, the bells ring just right,
While I juggle my thoughts, in pure, silly flight.

A jar filled with questions, no answers survive,
Yet here in the moment, oh, how I thrive!
Life's comic relief, in colors so bright,
As I chase down the silliest thoughts of the night.

So let's toast to confusion and embrace all the fun,
A life without meaning is simply well-spun.
With chuckles and chaos, we'll paint this sweet tale,
In moments unbound, we'll always prevail!

A Journey Without a Compass

With no map in hand, I just roam,
Lost in this world, feels like home.
I trip on paths I never planned,
But laughter fills my clumsy stand.

I ask for directions, they just smile,
They've lost their way, it's been a while.
I dance in circles, round and round,
What fun to not know where I'm bound!

The stars above, they twinkle bright,
Guide me gently in the night.
I don't need a compass, it's a hoot,
To wander free in this silly pursuit.

Each day's a gift I unwrap with glee,
Who needs the weight of certainty?
I'll frolic here, carefree and spry,
Living life with a twinkling eye.

Blissful Ignorance of Destiny's Map

Woke up this morning, scratched my head,
No clue on where my dreams were led.
I brewed my coffee, spilled some too,
A messy start? I'll go for two!

Maps of life all look the same,
A cryptic puzzle, a guessing game.
I draw a line and then I veer,
Oh look, there's whimsy over here!

With no agenda, I dance through days,
In joyous tunes that life displays.
The questions linger, like a fun parade,
Who really cares? We'll make the grade!

So here I am, a joyful chap,
Sipping bliss from fate's own lap.
In this grand circus, I'll just play,
Because not knowing makes for a bright day!

The Art of Living Without Answers

Why search for answers, I often think,
When life's a canvas, paint it pink.
I chase the shadows, I ride the breeze,
Tickle the stars, dance with the trees.

Philosophers ponder with furrowed brow,
While I giggle and take a bow.
Unraveled mysteries, I leave alone,
For riddle-filled life is my comfort zone.

Dinner's served but I skipped the meal,
Too busy tasting what joy can feel.
With every guess, a chuckle shared,
In a riddle of life, I'm blissfully scared.

So hand me a question, I'll spin it around,
In a world unscripted, laughter is found.
Life unexamined is a sprint and a spree,
Embracing the chaos, it's just me!

Happy Wanderer in a Sea of Mysteries

Oh me, oh my, where shall I tread?
In salty seas or up a thread?
With waves of joy that crash and play,
I float along, come what may.

The mysteries swirl like a vibrant dance,
I throw my hat, give fate a chance.
A curious mind, a cheeky grin,
Oh where to next? Let's begin!

I sip on doubts like fine old wine,
Each drop a giggle, simply divine.
For in the unknown, there's room to play,
In a whimsical world, I'll laugh all day.

So tide me over with splashes of cheer,
Each wave a giggle, no hint of fear.
I'll skip along this cosmic spree,
A happy wanderer, wild and free.

Floating in Infinite Possibilities

I woke up this morning, no clue in my head,
Like socks in a dryer, my thoughts all misled.
What's the point of the coffee? Does it even matter?
Maybe life's a big joke — who'd dare try to flatter?

I skipped breakfast, who needs toast?
Life's like a piñata, just swing and be ghost.
The sun may be shining, the rain may come too,
But really, who cares? I'll just dance with the dew.

Maps? Oh, I've tossed them, why follow a path?
Each twist is delightful, it's equivalent math.
I'll spiral through cosmos, or maybe a mall,
In this wacky amusement, I'll joyfully sprawl.

Life might be a riddle, or a colorful mess,
I'll wear it like confetti, I must confess.
So here's to the chaos, the laughs that ensue,
With wonder as my guide, I'll just wing it anew.

Serenity Found in Questions' Embrace

Questions abound like loose shopping carts,
Rolling through my mind, they tickle my smarts.
What's the point of ducks? Or socks without pairs?
In this vast sea of wonders, I'm swimming on airs.

I ponder the why's as I munch on some cheese,
Is cheese just a question? Or should I say please?
Life spins like a top, and I'm caught in the dance,
With giggles surrounding, I'll just leave it to chance.

A book with no answers, I flipped it today,
Each page just confused me, so I stuffed it away.
The universe chuckles, a mischief-filled laugh,
In the land of uncertainty, let's take a nice gaff.

So let's toast to queries, in hues oh so bright,
And revel in laughter, like stars in the night.
With silliness guiding our whimsical quest,
In questions we flourish, in jest we find rest.

The Universe of Lost Knowings

I searched for the answers, found a pair of shoes,
But no cosmic clues, just yesterday's news.
What is the secret? Oh, lost in the fray,
Just rolling through life, in a comical way.

The stars in the sky wink, they know more than me,
But they're too busy twinkling, carefree and free.
With marshmallow fluff clouds above my head, so high,
I'll embrace the confusion, and try not to cry.

With a frown and a giggle, I tripped on a thought,
Life's puzzles are funny, perplexing but hot.
I'll wear mismatched socks as I skip down the lane,
In a universe bursting with silly disdain.

So here's to the lost ones, the whys and the what's,
We'll dance through the dark, lose our tattered knots.
With laughter our guide in this colorful race,
We'll cherish the chaos, in a joyous embrace.

Echoes of Joy in the Unknown

In a realm full of echo, where answers just fade,
I giggle at questions, like a playful charade.
What's the sum of my worries? A whole lot of fun,
I'll chase my own shadow, until life's done.

As clocks run backwards, I'll move with the breeze,
And juggle my thoughts like they're fluffy fresh peas.
Unraveling mysteries wrapped tight like a bow,
I'll find joy in the snags, let the giggles flow.

If life's a big puzzle that's missing a piece,
I'll dance through the gaps, find my funky release.
Each moment's a riddle, a laugh in disguise,
With a wiggle and wobble, I'll reach for the skies.

So gather your smiles, let's revel tonight,
In this carousel cosmic, so dizzy and bright.
For within every jest lies a glimmering truth,
In the unknown we blossom, reclaiming our youth.

Heartbeats in the Absence of Answers

In a world where questions play,
I trip on doubts each day.
A goat once told me to relax,
But it chewed my favorite snacks.

Why does bread always hit the floor?
Is life a cosmic grocery store?
My socks seem lost in space and time,
I wear one blue, the other lime.

Searching high and digging low,
I found a cat that didn't know.
He winked and we both had a laugh,
As we pondered life's impossible math.

So I dance with blissful dismay,
In this surreal and silly play.
Embracing confusion, I cheer,
For clarity's just not my career.

The Beauty of Unfathomable Horizons

Out here where the wild things roam,
I ponder if I'm lost or home.
Birds chirp tales, I can't decode,
Yet I skip through life like a little toad.

A tree once whispered secrets loud,
While I stood there, feeling proud.
Its bark just chuckled at my quest,
Oh, how I adore this silly jest!

Mist is thick and fog's my friend,
With every turn, I just pretend.
The sun plays peek-a-boo with clouds,
As I chase whims, lost in crowds.

So here's to the paths that lead nowhere,
And shoes that embrace the fresh air.
In the unknown, I find delight,
Laughing madly through day and night.

Embracing the Unfathomable

With a smile that defies the clock,
I wear mismatch shoes, more fun to rock.
Life's puzzles may have missing bits,
Yet I float through chaos with little fits.

A cloud told me, don't think too hard,
I should plant flowers in my yard.
The flowers giggled, who needs a rule?
Let's start a dance party, that's way cool!

I asked a snail about the end,
He shrugged and just offered a friend.
With a shell like a mini spaceship,
Together we took a wild trip.

In this realm of shaped confetti,
Where life's a joke, and that's quite heady.
I twirl and laugh with every chance,
Until the universe joins the dance.

Dancing in the Void

In the void where questions prance,
I found a frog who loved to dance.
He hopped on boulders, quite the sight,
Under stars that twinkled bright.

Why do socks escape the wash?
Befuddles my mind, like a bad nosh!
But here in nothing, I can spin,
Embracing chaos, my little win.

A whisper said to chase my tail,
So I ran like a ship set sail.
Around and around, what's the point?
Laughing hard—my favorite joint!

With cosmic giggles and joyful shouts,
I dance with purpose, sans all doubts.
In the void, hilarity reigns,
Life's absent answers—what a gain!

The Colorful Spectrum of Unfamiliarity

In a world painted in shades of surprise,
We trip on bananas and giggle with sighs.
The map says 'home,' but we lost our way,
Still dancing in circles, we're here for the play.

With questions like confetti that float through the air,
Each thought is a puzzle, a whimsical scare.
Why do ducks quack? Why do clouds feel light?
We laugh at the limits of reason and sight.

The universe winks in its colorful tones,
As we trip over thoughts like we're dancing on stones.
Embracing the silly, with purpose amiss,
We toast to confusion, and laugh with a twist.

So here's to the laughter that bubbles and flows,
In a life full of moments where mystery grows.
Like socks that get lost in the game of the spin,
We find joy in the absurd, let the party begin!

Playful Curiosity in an Infinite Sky

In a sky full of questions, we float on a kite,
With paperclip dreams that take off in the night.
We chase after answers like puppies at play,
But every lost clue just leads us away.

Why do stars twinkle? What's under the sea?
With laughter as fuel, we're as wild as can be.
The wind tells a story that tickles our ears,
As we jump into puddles of giggles and cheers.

With a secretive grin, the day offers fun,
As we dive into mysteries, one by one.
Like spaghetti that dances off plates in the rain,
The magic of not knowing is never in vain.

So let's pack up our wonders and chase them around,
In the infinite sky, where nonsense is found.
With a wink and a smile, we'll soar ever high,
In this playful curiosity, we're destined to fly!

A Diary of Wonder and Whimsy

On the first page of nonsense, the story begins,
Where shoes walk in circles and socks sprout fins.
A cat that can sing and a dog on a swing,
In the diary of whimsy, we write down everything.

Each doodle is silly, with splashes of cheer,
As we ponder the universe over vanilla beer.
Why does the moon wear such a bright, goofy grin?
It knows that confusion is how we all win!

The plot has no outline; it dances with glee,
With plot twists like noodles that wiggle and flee.
We scribble in laughter, we doodle in rhyme,
In this book of the wacky, there's no sense of time.

So here's to the pages that crinkle and fold,
Filled with sunshine, and stories retold.
In this whimsical journey of joy and surprise,
We celebrate the quirky, with joy in our eyes!

Bubbles of Laughter in a Cloud of Mystery

Floating on bubbles of laughter so light,
With giggles that shimmer like stars in the night.
What's hiding behind all these curious thoughts?
A circus of wonders that no one ever bought.

Like candy-floss clouds that dance in the sky,
We bounce on the whims like a butterfly.
Why do toasters toast only on the sly?
With every silly question, we give it a try!

Each bubble that pops brings another surprise,
As we chase after riddles with wide-open eyes.
The joy of the unknown floats high in the air,
Like jelly beans dancing without a care.

So here in the laughter, the mystery swells,
In clouds of confusion, we ring our own bells.
With bubbles of joy in this life that we find,
We celebrate laughter, and leave reason behind!

Kaleidoscope of Unanswered Dreams

In a swirl of colors bright,
I chase my thoughts like butterflies.
Each twist and turn, a new delight,
As logic's map simply defies.

I ask the moon why it is round,
It giggles back, then winks away.
The questions dance, yet never found,
I laugh aloud—come join the play!

With tangled thoughts in jumbled glee,
My coffee's cold, I've lost my way.
Unraveling threads, wild and free,
Perhaps it's best I choose to stray.

So here I stand, delightfully lost,
Where sense is scarce, yet joy runs wild.
Adventures bloom, no matter the cost,
In this mad garden, I'm just a child.

Serendipity in the Unfamiliar

I tripped on thoughts like scattered seeds,
Each landed spot, a chance surprise.
A dance of fate, embracing leads,
With every tumble, laughter flies.

I ponder fish that climb up trees,
And squirrels that skateboard through air.
Life's a circus, no guarantees,
Yet in the chaos, I'll declare!

Hiccups in wisdom, drops of fun,
Smiles sprout like dandelions.
I chase the sun on a bicycle run,
And end up wrapped in capybaras.

In every blunder, I find a spark,
A gleeful shrug, a wink, a grin.
The world's a maze, with a goofy arc,
Where every mistake is where I begin.

Laughter Beneath the Stars of Ambiguity

Under starlit skies, so vast,
I ponder why ducks wear bow ties.
The midnight dance, shadows cast,
With giggles soft as fireflies.

I greet confusion with a cheer,
A playful nod to fate's sly jest.
In mystery's grip, I have no fear,
For every question's just a quest!

The cosmos spins a silly yarn,
With planets that waltz on tightropes.
I float along, no cause for alarm,
In dreams that bubble, laugh, and elope.

So here's to mysteries, laughter loud,
In the grand cosmic game of chance.
Let's twirl and leap, a joyous crowd,
For not knowing—what a wild dance!

Wonders Unbound in Endless Search

I stroll through fields of questions wide,
Where answers play hide-and-seek.
A rabbit with a top hat strides,
He murmurs secrets, "Take a peek!"

Curiosity runs amok,
Like kittens tripping on their paws.
I chuckle as my thoughts unlock,
With silly dreams that never pause.

What's life but a carnival of jest?
A sweet parade of quirky sights.
Each misstep leads to another quest,
With giggles shared in starry nights.

So here I wander, blissfully lost,
In this circus where wonders bloom.
Embracing fun, no matter the cost,
I'll find my joy in every room.

Murmurs of Solitude and Wonder

In the garden of thought, I wander wide,
Each flower a thought, where dreams abide.
A bee buzzes by, it's lost in the chase,
With no clue of purpose, just joy on its face.

The sky wears a hat made of whims and of grace,
Chasing clouds like the rabbit, oh what a race!
I giggle at stars that blink with delight,
They twinkle and tease, keeping secrets at night.

Why fret about answers when questions are fun?
To dance with the unknown, oh what a run!
With a shimmy and shake, I join in the spree,
Life's riddle wrapped in absurdity.

Like socks in the dryer, I'm twisted and spun,
Embracing the chaos, it feels like a pun.
Who needs a map for this whimsical ride?
In the land of the clueless, I take the glide.

The Bliss of Not Knowing

Oh my brain's a piñata, spill candy and dreams,
With bits of confetti and wild, silly schemes.
What's life? A riddle, or maybe a joke,
As I scratch my head while I wobble and poke.

I trip on the questions, fall flat on my face,
But laughter erupts, takes me to a new place.
A puzzle unsolved is a puzzle that's grand,
With joy in the mystery, I leap and I stand.

The clock ticks on softly, its hands play a game,
Tickling my senses, forgetting my name.
Does it matter at all if I miss all the signs?
I skip through existence, dancing on lines.

So here's to the chaos and galas of fate,
The thrill of the clueless, it's never too late.
With you by my side, we'll laugh till we glow,
In a world of 'Just why?' we'll frolic and flow.

Escaping the Chains of Definition

Why box up the sunshine? It's brighter than that,
Let's lounge with the shadows and dance with the cat.
What's 'purpose'? A riddle, as thin as a sigh,
So I'll flit like a firefly, tickling the sky.

A salad of notions, tossed high in the air,
With croutons of chaos and dressing of flair.
I snatch at the questions like bubbles on wine,
And relish the laughter, it's utterly fine.

So come join the circus with no exit signs,
With clowns full of wisdom, in clown shoes and fines.
We'll juggle our worries, they'll bounce off the floor,
In the circus of life, who could ask for more?

Let's weave joy from confusion, a tapestry bright,
In the land of the wobbly we'll take our delight.
With every lost reason, we'll cheer and we'll shout,
In the chains of 'defining,' we'll wiggle right out.

Joyride Through the Abyss

I've hopped on a comet and cranked up the tunes,
With stardust for wheels, howling wild to the moons.
What's down there, you ask? I'm not really sure,
But who needs directions when adventure's the lure?

We dodged through the questions like asteroids whizzing,
With giggles and grins, this joyride's a blizzing.
Each twist in the plot, an unexpected surprise,
Life's a comic book where the funny parts rise.

The abyss is a canvas, so let's throw some paint,
With colors of nonsense, and whims that are quaint.
As I careen through the dark, with laughter so bright,
I discover the magic embedded in night.

So here's to the thrill of the not knowing words,
Like singing to cats or conversing with birds.
We're cruising forever, a nonsensical drift,
With every "why not?", we uncover the gift.

Sailing on a Sea of Ambiguity

With a compass that points any way,
We sail and laugh, come what may.
Waves of questions, sails of delight,
Navigating nonsense by day and by night.

The map is a jigsaw with missing pieces,
Each port's a riddle that never ceases.
We sip on confusion, toast to the unknown,
In this quirky adventure, we're never alone.

Lost at sea, but what's the fuss?
The stars above sing songs for us.
Waves tickle our boat, with splashes of glee,
Embracing the chaos, wild and free.

In this ocean of whims, we dive with a grin,
Chasing the whims, where the fun begins.
So here's to the journeys with no end in sight,
Riding the waves of pure delight.

Joy in the Question

Why are we here? A query so grand,
With laughter and wonder, we make our stand.
Twirling in circles, like leaves in a breeze,
Finding glee in the puzzled unease.

Do ducks know their purpose? I doubt it so much,
As they quack and they waddle, their lives never hush.
We ponder, we chuckle, we jump and we spin,
In the search for an answer, where do we begin?

With each silly question, a giggle takes flight,
It's the playful confusion that feels just right.
Like kids in a sandbox, with shovels and dreams,
We build castles of laughter, or so it seems.

What if tomorrow brings marshmallow rain?
Would we dance through the puddles, again and again?
In the land of inquiry, we're kings and queens,
Reveling in jest, fulfilling our dreams.

Celebrating the Inconclusive

Raise a glass to the vague and unclear,
To the things we don't know, we give a cheer!
In riddles we trust, like a dog with a bone,
In a world full of questions, we're never alone.

With pies made of clouds and soup made of stars,
We journey through life in our whimsical cars.
Each fork in the road, a punchline in disguise,
We chuckle at fate with our quirky replies.

Confusion is sweet, like candy from trees,
It tickles our tongues, soaring like the breeze.
So let's bake a cake with a sprinkle of doubt,
And party in realms where certainties pout.

For what's life without giggles in the dark?
A quest without joy, with no sparkle or spark!
So here's to the puzzles, the jests, and the fun,
In the dance of the unknown, we've only begun!

Playful Hearts in the Dark

In shadows we frolic, with glee like a kite,
Where questions run wild and the stars look just right.
With a wink and a laugh, we embrace the unknown,
In the theater of night, we make it our own.

Why are we here? Who really will know?
Let's twirl in the moonlight, let laughter flow.
With stardust on our shoes, we jump and we dive,
In the joy of uncertainty, we truly feel alive.

The clock ticks absurdly, in its twisted design,
As we dance on the edge of the cosmic line.
Each heartbeat a question, a riddle, a game,
With chuckles and giggles, we never feel shame.

So let's play in the dark, with our hearts set aglow,
In the beauty of not knowing, we let our spirits flow.
With hearts intertwined, we shun all the fuss,
In this festival of fun, it's just you and us.

The Delight of Questioning Everything

Why is the sky so blue, I wonder,
While squirrels plot their daily plunder?
Do fish know their names in the sea?
Or do they just swim, wild and free?

Why do socks disappear, it's a crime!
Do they dance with the dust bunnies in time?
Is laughter just a tickle in disguise?
Or a secret shared between our sighs?

If cows had a throne, would they reign supreme?
Or daydream of fields in a starry gleam?
Do we need answers or simply a laugh?
As we chase shadows down a sunny path?

So I munch on my snacks, lost in thought,
As questions float and answers are sought.
Is this life a riddle wrapped in a song?
Maybe it's just where the quirky belong!

A Symphony of Undefined Moments

In the morning sun, the toast pops high,
Do burnt edges have feelings? Oh my!
The kettle whistling, a strange little tune,
As I ponder if ducks can carry the moon.

Is cereal in milk really a stew?
And what's a cat thinking? It's such a goo!
Do leaves gossip as they flutter down?
Or is it just whispers from the grass, "Wear a crown?"

People juggle ideas, I juggle my keys,
As clouds float by like wanderers at ease.
Are the ants plotting world domination today?
Or are they just trying to find their way?

With giggles and wiggles, the fridge gives a hum,
As I tiptoe through questions, my mind's a drum.
In this wild symphony, no answers suggest,
That maybe it's fun to simply guess!

The Enchantment of Wandering Thoughts

A butterfly lands, what does it recall?
Is it mapping adventures or dreaming small?
Do clouds compete for the fluffiest spot?
Or are they just dawdling, forgotten, forgot?

In the garden of whimsy, weeds grow tall,
Do they laugh when they trip or take a fall?
Is the moon a giant cookie on high?
And what about stars, do they just wink and fly?

With every tick-tock, I ponder and grin,
Does my pen have secrets? Oh, where do I begin?
Do fish discuss the currents' new style?
Or do they just swim and hang for a while?

Through the maze of musings, I meander along,
With a heart full of giggles and a head full of song.
Life is a puzzle, but who's keeping score?
Perhaps in the not-knowing, there's always more!

Finding Zen in a World of Chaos

In a cluttered room, my cat claims the chair,
Is he meditating or just plotting a scare?
Spilled coffee patterns paint thoughts anew,
Is the carpet a canvas in say, a zoo?

Bubble baths with rubber ducks in a row,
Are they having meetings that I don't know?
The clock ticks loudly, a rhythmic ballet,
Is it warning me time is running away?

With chaos surrounding, I stop and I smile,
As socks slide wrinkled across every mile.
Do dreams squeak when they pop like a balloon?
Or do they giggle and float 'til the moon?

Finding stillness in nonsense can be quite an art,
With laughter as the brush and wonder a part.
In this whirlwind of curious cheer,
The mystery of life feels deliciously near!

Questions Without Answers

Why do ducks have feathers, they waddle and quack?
Is there a map for life, or just stay on track?
Why do socks disappear, like magic, they flee?
Perhaps they're on holiday, sipping sweet tea.

Can cheese really dance, or is that just a dream?
Do ants have a day job, or are they a team?
What if clouds are pillows, soft in the sky?
Do stars play chess, or just wink as they fly?

Is time just a game with no rules to abide?
Is the moon just a cookie our hearts got to hide?
If laughter's contagious, can it spread through a wink?
Or maybe it's real, and we just have to think?

In a world full of questions, who's keeping the score?
What if spaghetti really lets dreams out the door?
So let's toss our worries, and dance out of line,
For answers are funny, when life's a punchline.

Wonder in Shadows

Do shadows have feelings, or just lurk and creep?
Is laughter a secret that whispers in sleep?
What if the sun is just playing a game?
And the moon chases fireflies for fortune and fame?

Are turtles just trucks with a built-in retreat?
Can laughter be measured, or just feel so sweet?
If trees like to dance when the wind hums a tune,
Are flowers just giggles that burst into bloom?

What if the stars just enjoy the loud night?
Do cats hold debates on how to take flight?
Can tickles be bottled, or do they escape?
And does time wear a hat, or just shape-shift and drape?

In a world of confusion where fun seems to reign,
Let's pretend we're clueless, and enjoy the train!
No maps or compasses needed today,
Just whispers of wonder in light-hearted play.

Laughing with Uncertainty

Do fish think of water, or just float in bliss?
Can rabbits hold meetings to plan their next miss?
Why do old shoes seem to collect all the dust?
Maybe they're dreaming of journeys or bust!

What if the fridge is alive with a hum?
Does it laugh at our choices, or just keep them numb?
Are clouds really marshmallows drifting on high?
And what if the sun turns out to be shy?

Can giggles grow wings or simply stay still?
Is there a contest for the best kind of thrill?
Do stars keep tallies on wishes we share?
And does the night giggle when we say a prayer?

In a whirlwind of nonsense where laughter resides,
Let's chase after wonders, let curiosity guide!
With questions so silly, who cares if they're true?
For laughter's the treasure that brightens our view!

The Freedom of Blank Pages

What's written on blankness, is it deep or just wild?
Do crayons hold secrets, or just dreams of a child?
If pencils could chatter, what tales would they tell?
Or maybe they'd giggle and say, "Oh, so swell!"

Are erasers just friends who help clear the gray?
Do markers have parties to color the day?
What if a doodle could dance on its own?
And chalk draws adventures on paths yet unknown?

If blank pages whisper, what do they intend?
Could laughter be lurking, around every bend?
Are thoughts just balloons that float high in the air?
Or are they confetti that we're free to share?

With ink, dreams can tumble and fumble about,
Each line tells a story, even when there's doubt!
So let's scribble and chuckle till worries all fade,
In the freedom of pages, let whimsy be played!

Curiosity Without Destination

I wander through the fields of thought,
With questions dancing, never caught.
Why is the sky so blue today?
Maybe it's just its playful way.

A map of life? I tossed it high,
It floated off like a butterfly.
Do socks have purpose, or just a flair?
I love their colors, beyond compare.

The cat next door pretends to know,
But he's just chasing shadows, though.
What's the secret to the universe?
Maybe it's just a giant purse.

So let's poke fun at the grand design,
And sip our tea, feeling just fine.
For in this game of guess and cheer,
Ignorance can sometimes feel like beer.

Wandering Through the Enigma

A riddle wrapped in layers thick,
I step right in, and take a pick.
What if life's a giant jest?
I giggle hard; I'm blessed, I guess.

The sun is shining, oh what a tease,
Like a riddle whispered by the breeze.
I chase the clouds, yet can't quite touch,
Maybe this world just likes to clutch.

The stars overhead chuckle low,
Why do they glow? No one can know!
I shrug my shoulders, enter the chase,
As laughter dances in empty space.

Wandering through this puzzling maze,
I break for snacks; I savor those rays.
Each twist and turn spinning the tale,
In this circus, I'll never fail.

Sweet Simplicity of Ignorance

Life's a jigsaw, missing a piece,
Yet here I am, savoring the fleece.
The why and wherefore twist and twirl,
A world of candy, a bright swirl.

Count the jellybeans? What a chore!
What if they're just a mythical store?
I taste the sweetness, not the math,
In this lifetime's delightful path.

Oh, who needs maps or perfect plans?
I prefer to dance in mismatched pants.
With giggles swirling through the air,
Ignorance, my friend, takes me anywhere.

So pass the donuts, skip the plight,
In this simple joy, life feels just right.
The laughter echoes, bright and clear,
In sweet simplicity, I persevere.

The Melody of Uncertainty

Life's a song with no clear note,
I hum along, just on my boat.
What makes a beat? It doesn't matter,
My giggles echo, louder than chatter.

A dance of ducks, a waddle wrong,
They quack along to our silly song.
Life's a tune played off-key,
But I'll join in, wild and free.

What's that tune in the distance, so bright?
Could it be joy, or just a kite?
With every twirl, I brings a grin,
Uncertainty lets the fun begin.

So welcome the chaos, it's quite the spree,
With every note, I'm who I'll be.
Life's melody, sweet and absurd,
In this strange dance, I sing unheard.

Whispers of Uncertainty

In a world where answers flee,
I dance with questions joyfully.
Why is the sky so blue today?
Perhaps it's just paint, who can say?

I tried to catch a flying thought,
But it slipped away, as I sought.
Where do socks vanish, oh so sly?
I suspect they're off to fun, oh my!

Life's puzzle, pieces all askew,
I laugh at clues I never knew.
Why does candy taste so sweet?
Maybe because it's a special treat!

So here I stand, arms open wide,
In a circus where mysteries abide.
The fun is found in the great unknown,
With jokes and jigs, I've brightly grown.

Dancing in the Shadows of Inquiry

Questions twirl like leaves in fall,
Each one a joke that tickles, enthralls.
Who invented socks, I do ponder,
Maybe a cat, just to cause wonder?

Laughter echoes in the dark,
As I leap around, a funny lark.
What's under my bed? The dust bunnies play,
Or perhaps a portal to worlds far away?

With each chuckle, fears fade to mist,
Is it really that hard to exist?
The answers bounce like a rubber ball,
Sometimes they're big, sometimes so small.

So I shimmy and giggle in the night,
Inviting the questions, dancing with light.
It's fun not to know, it's quite a thrill,
In the shadows of thought, time stands still.

Embracing the Beautiful Abyss

In the deep end where questions dive,
I find my laughter, I feel alive.
What's the meaning of this, I ask?
Perhaps it's just a curious task.

Floating on whims like a carefree sail,
With a grin, I embrace the surreal trail.
Why do ice creams melt on the ground?
Is it their way of dancing around?

Life's a riddle, beautifully absurd,
With giggles swirling, my thoughts stirred.
Why does the cat stare at the wall?
Maybe she hears the silly night's call.

So here I float in the cosmic sea,
Laughing at mysteries, happy and free.
In the delightful void where riddles reside,
I waltz with chaos, my joy can't hide.

The Freedom of Question Marks

I wander where the answers roam,
With questions like seeds, I've made my home.
What's the secret to a sunny day?
Could it be just the sky's playful way?

Like puppies chasing their own tails,
I follow each thought that never fails.
Why do we call it a 'kangaroo'?
I think it's just a sound that's fun to do!

In the forest of wonder, I laugh with glee,
Each query a leaf on the grand old tree.
What's for dinner? A mystery feast!
Where's my shoe? Maybe stuck to a beast!

So let's raise eyebrows, let all minds roam,
In the land of the lost, we'll feel at home.
With giggles and grins, we'll take our chance,
In the freedom of questions, let's all dance!

The Unseen Colors of Existence

Life's a circus, and I'm the clown,
With mismatched socks and a silly frown.
Paint splashes here, a dab there too,
Who needs a meaning? I'll eat my shoe!

The stars above twinkle in glee,
As I juggle questions, just wait and see.
With every tumble, a laugh comes out,
Life's a puzzle, but I'm not in doubt!

So roll with the punches, dance and sway,
The purpose? Who cares? Just seize the day!
With each odd turn, a chuckle we share,
In this wild ride, I haven't a care!

Puddles reflect a bright rainbow hue,
But what does it mean? I don't have a clue.
So let's skip and hop through this bizarre show,
The unseen colors are all that I know!

Frolicking in the Fields of Mystery

I wander through fields of questions wide,
With butterflies buzzing, they're my guide.
Chasing shadows and tickling the breeze,
Why fret on answers? I'll do as I please!

In the meadows, I'm a curious bee,
Sipping nectar of what might be.
Life's a riddle wrapped in a laugh,
I'll spin around and take my own path!

With wildflowers dancing, let me just say,
Understanding is overrated anyway!
The trees whisper secrets, but I'm not keen,
To unravel their tales, I'll just stay green!

So frolic with me through this grand charade,
In spaces unseen where meaning may fade.
Let's stomp in puddles, let's leap with glee,
For the joy in the question is truly the spree!

Radiance Beyond Understanding

I gaze at the sun, it winks at me,
What's its purpose? Who can decree?
Maybe it's shining just for my giggle,
Or playing a tune that makes me wiggle!

With stars in my eyes and a grin so wide,
I skip on clouds, let my heart be the guide.
In every stretch of this mysterious ride,
Who needs a reason when you're full of pride?

The moon's made of cheese or so they say,
But I'd trade a bite for a fun-filled day!
Questions are starlit roads we can roam,
In this riddle of life, I'm finally home.

So hoot like an owl, and dance like a fool,
In the radiance of joy, let's break all the rules.
What's the meaning? Let's shout a cheer,
In laughter and light, we have nothing to fear!

The Inheritance of Questions

Once upon a time, I found a big book,
Full of questions that made me look.
What's the point, and what's the plan?
Just pass the popcorn, let's watch the clowns!

I asked my pet goldfish, so wise and round,
"What is life, friend?" No answer was found.
It swam in circles, but still I giggled,
At the thought of wisdom that always tickles!

A tree spoke softly, "Just sway with the breeze,"
While squirrels laughed, climbing with ease.
The great mystery, a soft, silly song,
Tells me it's perfect to not know for long!

So let's toast our cups, filled with delight,
To questions inherited under starlight.
In this wild adventure with whimsy and cheer,
Not knowing is great, so let's persevere!

The Rapture of Questioning

Why do socks disappear, I ask,
Curse the washing machine's task.
Do ducks know they're quacking loud?
Life's absurdity makes me proud.

Is there a purpose in my snack?
Or is it just a donut track?
Do clouds giggle when they drift?
Oh, to ponder is a gift!

Why do we fry the things we bake?
Is there wisdom in the cake?
If I chase my tail like a dog,
Will I find truth in the fog?

Questions float like bubbles, fine,
Each pop reveals a new design.
Laughter echoes on the way,
In this chaos, I will stay.

Navigating by Stars of Curiosity

Stars twinkle like they know a joke,
I wish they'd share, but they just choke.
Why do we count the sheep to sleep?
Answers hide, like secrets deep.

Do fish get tired from swimming laps?
Are there mermaids trading maps?
Why do we all just scratch our heads?
With such questions, life spreads.

Do pillows dream of other beds?
Or do they find us in our heads?
What if time is just a game?
In this fun, you'll find no shame.

Sailing through thoughts, a curious boat,
Riddles cause my brain to float.
Every star a curious guide,
In weirdness, I take great pride.

Joy from the Uncharted Waters

In uncharted waters, I splash and play,
No compass needed for this ballet.
Why do ducks waddle and then quack?
Is there reason in their hack?

Do trees ever gossip with the breeze?
Or do they simply nod with ease?
If time stood still, would it get bored?
Such questions leave me clearly floored.

Why does cereal float like a boat?
What if dreams are just a note?
With laughter, I lose track of time,
In the unknown, I find my rhyme.

Every wave whispers a strange delight,
In this ocean of questions, I feel light.
Uncharted territories bring me glee,
In this madness, I am free.

Whimsy in the Face of Doubt

Why do I trip over my own shoes?
Is the earth playing tricks, or just the blues?
Do ants ever think they are giants?
In this world, joy defies silence.

What's the deal with a cat's lazy stare?
Do they ponder life, or not a care?
If life is a riddle wrapped in a puzzle,
Why do I burst out in chuckles?

Is the sky really blue, or just a ploy?
Do clouds conspire to steal my joy?
If I dance in circles, am I wise?
Or just a fool in a world of lies?

With whimsy and giggles, I weave my thread,
In a tapestry of questions, I tread.
Dive into doubt with a roaring cheer,
For the unknown holds nothing to fear.

Whispers of the Unknown

In the dark, the owls do jest,
What's the fuss? Who needs a quest?
Life's a riddle, twist and shout,
With snacks to share, there's no doubt.

Dancing socks upon the floor,
Worry not what's in store!
Follow butterflies to a feast,
Or create a sock puppet beast.

Questions float like silly balloons,
Life's a circus, playing tunes.
No answers needed, just some cheer,
With laughter ringing loud and clear.

So pluck the strings of joy and play,
A ticket to this grand ballet!
What's the point? Who really cares?
As long as we've got snacks to share!

Serenity in the Unexplored

In an ocean of jello, I find my peace,
With giggles and wobbles, my worries cease.
Uncharted lands where llamas roam,
Who needs a map when you feel at home?

Cupcake castles, frosting skies,
With jellybean rain that never lies.
What's the goal? Just bounce around,
In this frolicsome playground we've found.

Sailing boats made of candy clouds,
Where everyone laughs, and no one shrouds.
Life's a game — come join the fun,
Let's run through fields until we're done.

So smash the clock, let time stand still,
In this sweet chaos, we find our thrill.
What's the plan? We'll make it up,
As long as there's joy in our silly cup!

The Art of Being Lost

I took a stroll down Mystery Lane,
Passed a dancing llama without a brain.
With twinkling toes and a silly grin,
Who knew that chaos could feel like a win?

Maps are for those who seek a goal,
I'd rather just lounge and let the laughs roll.
In the mystery of not having a clue,
I find sweet bliss, how about you?

Frogs wearing hats join for tea,
Spilling stories as silly as can be.
With every hop, they dance and shout,
Lost in layers, that's what it's about!

So fear not the winding, twisted path,
With laughter as fuel, it always lasts.
In the art of getting lost, you see,
We find the joy, wild and free!

Beneath the Surface of Certainty

Beneath the surface, where confusion thrives,
A world of giggles, where nonsense dives.
Dancing raindrops with a twist of lime,
Who needs a reason when you can rhyme?

A fish in a top hat, sipping tea,
Asking questions, 'Who's really me?'
Life's a comedy, nothing quite plain,
With jellybean laughter ringing like rain.

Pancakes flying in the sunny skies,
Flipping fate with glazed-up pies.
Where answers hide and pranks take flight,
Let's revel in this silly delight!

So toss aside your rigid rules,
Embrace the fun, we're all just fools.
In chaos and charm, we find our way,
With gleeful hearts, it's time to play!

www.ingramcontent.com/pod-product-compliance
Lightning Source LLC
Chambersburg PA
CBHW072218070526
44585CB00015B/1385